Cover illustration: Two F-106A Delta Darts of the 194th Fighter Interceptor Squadron, California Air National Guard, scramble from Tyndall AFB (Air Force Base) for a 'William Tell' air defence meet mission.

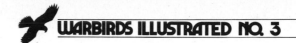

1. Six AGM-69A SRAM (Short-Range Attack Missile) weapons are carried on the starboard wing pylon of this B-52G from an unidentified Bomb Wing. The Stratofortress can carry 12 SRAMs underwing, and a further eight on a rotary launcher in the internal weapons bay. Lack of EVS (Electro-Optical Viewing System) indicates that this photograph dates back to about the mid-seventies. (USAF)

WARBIRDS ILLUSTRATED NO. 3

U.S. Air Force in the 1970s

LINDSAY T. PEACOCK

a&ap

ARMS AND ARMOUR PRESS

London—Melbourne—Harrisburg, Pa.

75 0258
75 0258

Introduction

In this third volume in the Warbirds Series, I have endeavoured to provide the reader with a selection of those aircraft and helicopter types which constituted the backbone of USAF air power during the seventies. Many are, of course, combat veterans, having seen extensive service in Vietnam, while some of the newer types, such as the F-15 Eagle and A-10 Thunderbolt, have yet to make their combat débuts. Despite this important distinction, I have attempted to treat old and new alike. Similarly, I make no apology for featuring transport and training aircraft, for these, too, have a vital part to play in maintaining US air power as a viable and effective entity.

Where possible, I have avoided using manufacturers' or USAF publicity photographs, preferring instead to draw upon my own files for the bulk of the illustrations. Consequently, very few have been published before, and I sincerely hope that readers will find the selection of interest and value.

Lindsay T. Peacock, 1982.

Warbird 3: US Air Force in the 1970s
Published in 1982 by
Arms and Armour Press, Lionel Leventhal Limited,
2-6 Hampstead High Street, London NW3 1QQ;
4-12 Tattersalls Lane, Melbourne, Victoria 3000, Australia;
Cameron and Kelker Streets, P.O. Box 1831, Harrisburg,
Pennsylvania 17105, USA

British Library Cataloguing in Publication Data:
Peacock, Lindsay
US Air Force in the 1970s.—Warbirds illustrated series; 3
1. United States. Air Force—Pictorial works
2. Aeroplanes, Military—History—Pictorial works
I. Title II. Series
623.74'6'0973 UG1243
ISBN 0-85368-438-3
Reprinted 1983

Layout by Anthony A. Evans.
Printed in Great Britain by William Clowes, Beccles, Limited.

2. This head-on view of one of the JAWS (Joint Attack Weapon System) A-10A Thunderbolt IIs shows to advantage the offset nose-wheel and the seven-barrelled Gatling-type cannon, which constitutes an integral part of the Thunderbolt's fearsome armoury.

▲3 ▼4

5▲

3. The first unit to convert to the latest variant of the McDonnell Douglas Eagle, the F-15C, was the 18th TFW (Tactical Fighter Wing) at Kadena, Okinawa, during the latter half of 1979. One of their initial deliveries is seen here returning to the flight line after a routine training mission. Note the practice AIM-9L Sidewinder missile mounted under the port wing.
4. The superlative visibility offered by the F-15's cockpit is clearly apparent in this view of the third production F-15C, which bears the markings of the 18th TFW. Note also the Vulcan M-61 cannon port in the wing root, and the lowered arrester hook.
5. Carrying a load of dummy AIM-7F Sparrow medium-range air-to-air missiles, the second prototype TF-15A taxies out to start a display routine at Farnborough. At that time it was proposed to adopt a basically light blue colour scheme on production Eagles, but this was later changed to varying tones of grey.
6. The ground crew prepare an F-15A of the 36th TFW for an air combat manoeuvring mission against the F-5E Tiger IIs of the Alconbury-based 527th TFTAS (Tactical Fighter Training Aggressor Squadron). Based at Bitburg, West Germany, the 36th previously operated F-4E Phantoms and is now in the process of re-equipping with the later F-15C variant of the Eagle.

6▼

▼7 ▲8

9▲

7. Another F-15A Eagle of the Bitburg-based 36th TFW displays the unusual wing planform to advantage in this fine study. The fairings and bulges at the top of the vertical tail surfaces are for electronic support measures equipment, such as radar warning receivers. (McDonnell Douglas)
8. The latest fighter aircraft to join the USAF is the General Dynamics F-16 Fighting Falcon, which now equips several US-based units and is shortly to be deployed overseas on a permanent basis for the first time. This F-16B, from the Armament Development Test Centre at Eglin AFB, carries Sidewinder missiles on the wing-tip rails and bomb racks on the underwing pylons.
9. Apart from the prototypes, the first F-16s to visit Europe were full-scale development examples which performed a practical operational evaluation in the late seventies. This F-16A carries rocket launchers, Sidewinder missiles and fuel tanks, and was photographed at Alconbury during the latter stages of the evaluation.

▲10 ▼11

10. The cannon port for the integral Vulcan M-61 20mm rotary cannon is readily apparent in this near head-on view of an F-16A Fighting Falcon. One of the small batch of FSD (Full-Scale Development) aircraft, it also features three external fuel tanks and wing-tip mounted AIM-9 Sidewinder air-to-air missiles. The pilot's excellent field of vision is a most noteworthy aspect of this type.

11. The first F-16B two-seater to be completed by the Belgian concern SABCA (Société Anonyme Belge de Constructions Aéronautiques) appeared at the 1979 Paris Air Show, where it proved to be one of the star attractions. The national flags of the five principal customers – USA, Belgium, Denmark, Holland and Norway – were displayed on the forward fuselage, and the US-allocated serial number 78-0162 was present on the fin. This aircraft was subsequently delivered to the Belgian Air Force. (General Dynamics)

12. The first of six F-16A FSD aircraft seen during the roll-out ceremonies at General Dynamics' Fort Worth facility. The colour scheme was basically red, white and blue. Once again, the flags of the five principal customers were carried on the nose section. Two two-seat F-16B FSD aircraft were also built. (General Dynamics)

13. Crewed-up and raring to go, this F-4D Phantom of the 18th TFW at Kadena, Okinawa, carries an SUU-16A gun pod on the centreline pylon and a Maverick electro-optically guided air-to-surface missile on the starboard inner wing pylon. Fuel tanks and an ALQ-119 jamming pod are also fitted.

GENERAL DYNAMICS
F-16
50745
USAF
U.S. AIR FORCE

12▲ 13▼

ZZ
505
RESCUE
7505

▲14 ▼15

14. With heat vapour obscuring the background, an RF-4C Phantom II of the 67th TRW (Tactical Reconnaissance Wing) taxies for take-off from Alconbury. A Westinghouse ALQ-119 jamming pod is present on the starboard inner wing pylon; also fitted are three large fuel tanks and a luggage container.
15. Seen during another European deployment, an RF-4C Phantom of the 363rd TRW operating from RAF Coltishall awaits its crew. A Tactical Air Command badge is displayed on the vertical tail, whilst the wing badge is present on the intake wall.
16. An RF-4C Phantom II of the Bergstrom-based 67th TRW undergoes 'last-chance' checks at Alconbury prior to beginning a transatlantic flight following European deployment. Note that both crew members have purposely lifted their hands out of the cockpit while the ground crew check the aircraft.
17. Part of the same Coltishall deployment seen in photograph 15, RF-4C 60474 of the 363rd TRW, prepares to land after a non-stop flight from Shaw AFB, South Carolina. The camera nose is clearly visible in this view, which also shows the leading edge flaps to advantage.
18. Backbone of the 17th Air Force in West Germany for many years, the F-4E Phantom is only now in the process of being replaced by the F-15 and F-16. This fearsome-looking shark-mouthed example is from the 86th TFW at Ramstein.

16▲ 17▼

18▼

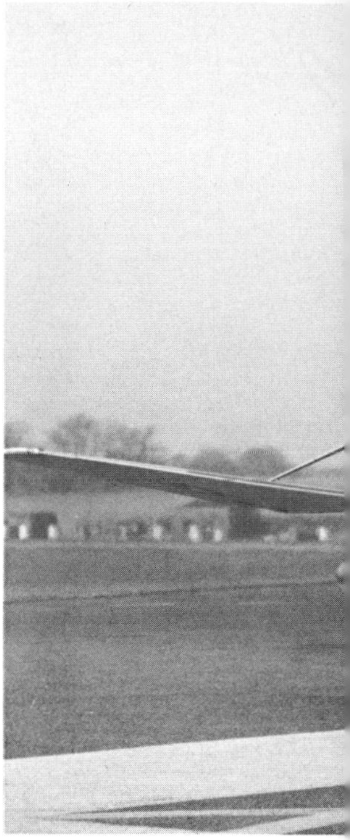

▲19 ▼20

19. A practice bomb dispenser, Maverick air-to-surface missile, ALQ-119 jamming pod and two external fuel tanks are carried by this heavily laden F-4D Phantom of the 18th Tactical Fighter Wing. Note also that the last four digits of the serial number (67709) are carried on a yellow patch at the bottom of the nose-wheel door.
20. The revised nose contours required to house the F-4E Phantom's integral Vulcan M-61 rotary cannon are evident in this view of a 50th TFW aircraft during the final stages of approach. Stationed at Hahn, West Germany, the 50th TFW began re-equipping with the F-16A Fighting Falcon during late 1981.
21. Formation strips are clearly visible on the nose, centre section and fin of this 81st TFW F-4D, seen taxiing at Bentwaters before the wing re-equipped with the A-10A. The infra-red sensor below the nose radome is also evident. (USAF)
22. Several ANG (Air National Guard) units now utilize variants of the Phantom in the pure interceptor rôle, almost all of which are finished in a grey overall 'air superiority' colour scheme. One such unit is the 171st FIS (Fighter Interceptor Squadron) from Selfridge, Michigan, which uses a rather attractive black and yellow trim for its insignia.

21▲ 22▼

▲23 ▼24

▼25

23. The older and less sophisticated F-105B model of the Thunderchief served with both the ANG and AFRES (Air Force Reserve) for much of the seventies. This machine carries the insignia of the 141st TFS, New Jersey ANG, and was stationed at McGuire AFB until the unit's recent conversion to the F-4D Phantom II. (Don Linn)
24. Among the last conventional F-105D Thunderchiefs to see service with front-line elements of the USAF were the handful that flew with the 57th Fighter Weapons Wing at Nellis AFB, Nevada. Thcsc were normally used to develop and evaluate new tactics and items of equipment.
25. An F-105D Thunderchief of the Air Force Reserve's 465th TFS (Tactical Fighter Squadron) touches down at Sculthorpe, England, after a non-stop transatlantic flight from Tinker AFB, Oklahoma, in 1978. The fin code letters 'SH' supposedly stood for 'Shit-Hot', by the way.
26. A blue dummy Sidewinder missile appears under the wing of this F-15A Eagle, seen on final approach to Mildenhall during 1979. The fin code combination 'CR' refers to the 32nd TFS at Soesterberg, Holland, which has recently completed conversion to the newer and more sophisticated F-15C model.
27. The red and white markings on the fin of this General Dynamics F-16B Fighting Falcon signify that it was assigned to the Armament Development Test Centre at Eglin AFB, Florida. An AIM-9 Sidewinder air-to-air missile is carried on the wing-tip rail, and a bomb rack is visible underwing.

26▲ 27▼

▲28 ▼29

30▲ 31▼

28. The more familiar tactical camouflage colour scheme is worn by this F-4E Phantom II of the 347th TFW at Moody AFB, Georgia. The Tactical Air Command badge is displayed on the fin. This aircraft also features the black code letters and serial data that became common during the late seventies; previously, they were presented in white.
29. Now one of the most effective weapons in the USAF inventory, the F-111 suffered from numerous problems during its development and early service career. This F-111E is from the 20th TFW at Upper Heyford and wears the standard F-111 finish of camouflaged upper surfaces with black undersides.
30. Another 'Thud' that took part in the 465th TFS's 1978 deployment was 91729, seen here soon after arrival at Sculthorpe. Flown by the Commanding Officer, it carried the name 'East Anglia Express' on the nose-wheel door. Note the MER (Multiple Ejection Rack) on the centreline stores station.
31. The last Thunderchiefs to see active service with the Air Force's front-line were the F-105G 'Wild Weasels' of the 35th TFW at George AFB, California. Essentially a modification of the two-seat F-105F they were used extensively in Vietnam in the SAM-suppression rôle. In this photograph, the fairings for the integral jamming system are visible below the wing root intakes, and a rocket launcher is carried on the centreline pylon.

▲32 ▼33

32. A brace of F-106A Delta Darts from the 194th FIS, California ANG, scramble for a simulated interception exercise over the air combat range adjacent to Tyndall AFB, Florida.
33. With the cockpit open and dragging its braking parachute, an F-106A Delta Dart of the 49th FIS returns to dispersal after completing a mission in the 'William Tell' weapons meeting. Antennae for the SAGE (Semi-Automated Ground Environment) control system are visible below the aft fuselage.
34. The clean lines of the Delta Dart are particularly apparent in this view of an aircraft from the 194th FIS. Note the presence of an ACMI (Air Combat Manoeuvring Instrumentation) pod under the starboard wing, and the infra-red sensor fairing directly ahead of the cockpit.
35. Five ANG fighter squadrons currently use the Delta Dart. The example pictured here is operated by the 101st FIS from Otis ANGB, Massachusetts. Its colours are predominantly pale blue and white.

34▲ 35▼

▲36 ▼37

36. Like most of its contemporaries, the F-100 Super Sabre spent the final years of its service life with second-line units, such as the Texas ANG's 182nd TFS. Fin markings on the aircraft seen here at Edwards AFB in late 1978 consisted of a red band with the name of the state superimposed in white.
37. Peeling paintwork around the aft fuselage was a common feature of all Super Sabres and is well illustrated by this 20th TFW F-100F two-seater. A noteworthy feature of this aircraft is the blind-flying hood, used for instrument training flights, in the rear cockpit.
38. The last fully operational USAF unit to operate the Super Sabre was the 48th TFW at Lakenheath, England. This F-100D bears the 'LS' code-letter combination of the 493rd TFS, which was one of three squadrons assigned to that Fighter Wing.
39. McDonnell's F-101B Voodoo now survives in just a handful of ANG Fighter Interceptor Squadrons and the Air Defence Weapons Centre. This example belongs to the 136th FIS at Niagara Falls, New York. The fairing directly ahead of the cockpit houses the sensor for the Infra-Red Search and Tracking System.
40. An F-101B Voodoo of the Air Defence Weapons Centre taxies out for a mission on the fully instrumented air combat manoeuvring range near Tyndall AFB. An ACMI pod is carried below the forward fuselage, but this machine does not feature an infra-red sensor housing.

38▲ 39▼

40▼

▲41 ▼42

43▲

41. In addition to the interceptor variant, the Voodoo also provided sterling service in the reconnaissance rôle, for which it was produced as the RF-101A and RF-101C. The camera nose, which was a standard feature of both sub-types, is clearly visible in this view of an RF-101C from the 66th TRW at Upper Heyford.
42. With the drag chute trailing and the air brakes deployed, an F-101B of the Air Defence Weapons Centre returns to Tyndall AFB. No infra-red sensor is fitted to this Voodoo, which has dark blue main undercarriage doors. Note also that only the forward cockpit is occupied.
43. Voodoos from the 'Lone Star' state. Four F-101Fs of the 111th FIS at Ellington AFB, Texas, fly in formation near their home base. Notable features are the SAGE (Semi-Automated Ground Environment) antenna under the aft fuselage, the black wing-walk areas, and the Bicentennial trim above the centre fuselage section. The F-101F was essentially a dual-control trainer version of the basic F-101B interceptor. (USAF)

FLA
0-61421
FLA
U.S. AIR FORCE

▲44 ▼45

CALIFORNIA
61474
U.S. AIR FORCE
163

▼46

CALIFORNIA
61329
CALIFORNIA
61450
CALIFORNIA
U.S. AIR FORCE
163

44. Another 'Century Series' fighter that was extensively used by the Air National Guard was the Convair F-102A Delta Dagger. These examples belong to the 159th FIS at Jacksonville International Airport, Florida. The trusty 'Deuce' was not destined to see out the decade, apart from as the PQM-102 pilotless target drone.
45. A nearby mountain range provides a fine backdrop for an F-102A Delta Dagger of the 196th FIS, California ANG, during 1973. The open weapon bay and missile rails are easily seen below the centre fuselage section.

46. Four 'Deuces' of the 196th FIS rest at Ontario, California, between routine training missions. Three are in the standard grey overall finish applied to interceptors, whilst the aircraft second from the left wears a most distinctive natural metal colour scheme.
47. Overseas-based F-102A Delta Daggers, such as this aircraft of the 496th FIS at Hahn, West Germany, all gained camouflage battledress in the latter half of the sixties and very few ever wore unit insignia. The bulbous object directly ahead of the cockpit is an infra-red sensor device.

47▲

▲48 ▼49

48. Apart from the Luftwaffe aircraft at Luke, very few Starfighters were active with the USAF in the seventies. This machine is one of a handful of F-104As that were in store at the start of the decade. Some later model F-104Cs operated with the Puerto Rico ANG's 198th TFS until about 1974.

49. Although it wears USAF titles and the 'star and bar' US national marking, this F-104G Starfighter is in fact a Luftwaffe aircraft operated by the 58th Tactical Fighter Training Wing from Luke AFB, Arizona, on pilot training duties.

50. Relatively few examples of the Republic F-84F Thunderstreak survived at the start of the seventies and these were quickly withdrawn after an accident caused by structural corrosion. The aircraft seen here, formerly of the Massachusetts ANG, continued to serve a useful purpose on ground instruction with the George T. Baker Aviation School in Miami, Florida.

51. Another stalwart that bowed out during the seventies was the F-86 Sabre. This F-86H was one of a substantial number passed to the US Navy's Naval Weapons Centre at China Lake, California, for use as QF-86H pilotless drone targets.

52. Most F-86 Sabres did, however, end their days at the Military Aircraft Storage and Disposition Centre (MASDC) at Davis-Monthan AFB, Arizona. This F-86H, last used by the 131st TFS Massachusetts ANG, was stored at MASDC for a while but was finally scrapped in the early seventies. The white patches around the fuselage and cockpit are a preserving material known as 'Spraylat'.

50▲ 51▼

52▼

▲53 ▼54

53. Like the McDonnell Douglas F-4 Phantom, Ling-Temco-Vought's Corsair was originally conceived for service with the United States Navy. The A-7D pictured here at Andrews AFB during September 1972 wears the colours and insignia of the 354th TFW's 353rd TFS from Myrtle Beach AFB, South Carolina.

54. One of the wildest colour schemes yet applied to the A-7D Corsair must surely have been that adorning 20223 of the 23rd TFW during the US Bicentennial year of 1976. This aircraft was basically white with red and blue trim. (C. Pocock)

55. Most of the early A-7D Corsairs progressed to the Air Force Systems Command after conclusion of the initial development programme. This machine, from the Air Force Flight Test Centre at Edwards AFB, was the second A-7D to be built and was used to test a specialized digital attack system in the late seventies. Note the absence of in-flight refuelling equipment.

56. Colloquially known as the 'Wart Hog', Fairchild-Republic's A-10A Thunderbolt II is unlikely to win any prizes in an aircraft beauty contest but is extremely efficient at 'killing' tanks. The aircraft seen here is finished in a special colour scheme evaluated as part of the JAWS (Joint Attack Weapon System) project in the latter half of the seventies.

55▲ 56▼

57. Hail and farewell! An F-4D Phantom II of the 81st TFW shares the Bentwaters apron with its replacement, the Fairchild-Republic A-10A Thunderbolt II. The latter is finished in the original basically grey colour scheme.
58. Some idea of the A-10A's massive weapons-carrying capability can be gained from this view of one of the prototypes during early development trials from Edwards AFB. In addition to conventional bombs, the Thunderbolt can also use 'Smart' weapons, such as the Maverick TV-guided air-to-surface missile. (Fairchild-Republic)
59. In addition to front-line USAF units, new production A-10As have also been delivered direct to four ANG units, replacing either the A-37B Dragonfly or the F-100D Super Sabre. A-10A 80647 of the 131st TFS, Massachusetts ANG, is seen here during refuelling at Tyndall AFB, Florida. Noteworthy features are the integral crew access ladder, and the massive belly fuel tank.

▲57 ▼58

59▲

▲60 ▼61

▼62

60. Another view of one of the specially marked JAWS Thunderbolt IIs operated by the 57th Fighter Weapons Wing from Nellis AFB, Nevada. The chequer-board marking on the fins is black and yellow.

61. The unit insignia visible on the nose of this F-111F is that of USAFE's 'Statue of Liberty' wing, namely the 48th TFW at RAF Lakenheath. Note that the weapons bay doors are in the open position, and that the aircraft carries a white practice bomb dispenser under the port wing.

62. In addition to the internal weapons bay, the F-111 is also capable of carrying a substantial amount of external ordnance. This F-111F of the 48th TFW features six folding-fin retarded bombs on one of the six underwing stores stations.

63. With the undercarriage partially retracted and smoke spewing from the eight J57 turbojet engines, a B-52D Stratofortress of the 96th Bomb Wing reaches for the sky at the start of a transatlantic flight to its home base at Dyess, Texas, after a brief deployment in Britain. This variant of the Stratofortress is unique in being the only member of the family to feature black undersides and fin surfaces.

64. With the undercarriage in the process of retracting, an 87th FIS F-106A Delta Dart gets airborne for a mission from Tyndall AFB during the 'William Tell' fighter weapons competition. The red band around the fuselage signifies that this aircraft is assigned to a flight commander.

63▲ 64▼

▲65 ▼66

67▲ 68▼

69▼

65. Another of the new weapons systems to join the USAF during the seventies was the Fairchild Republic A-10A Thunderbolt II, portrayed here by a 'lizard' camouflaged example of the 81st TFW at Bentwaters, England. This was the first overseas wing to receive the 'Wart Hog', as the aircraft is jocularly called.
66. Standard tactical battle-dress is worn by this C-130E of the 317th Tactical Airlift Wing. Note the low-visibility national insignia and Military Airlift Command titles that were introduced late in the seventies.
67. In addition to use as a tactical fighter, the F-111 also joined Strategic Air Command as the FB-111A. A total of 76 were built. The survivors still equip two Medium Bomb Wings, and they are compatible with SRAM. A slightly different camouflage scheme was adopted by the FB-111A and they also feature white undersides. This example is from the 509th Bomb Wing at Pease AFB, New Hampshire.
68. The assorted slats, flaps and other control surfaces of the F-111's wing are readily apparent in this almost head-on view of a 48th TFW F-111F.
69. The black undersides and leading edge fairings give the F-111 a most sinister appearance when viewed from the front. Noteworthy features are the large low-pressure tyres and the fully variable horizontal tail surfaces. This example is also carrying four Mk 83 1,000lb (450kg) bombs on the external store stations.

▲70 ▼71

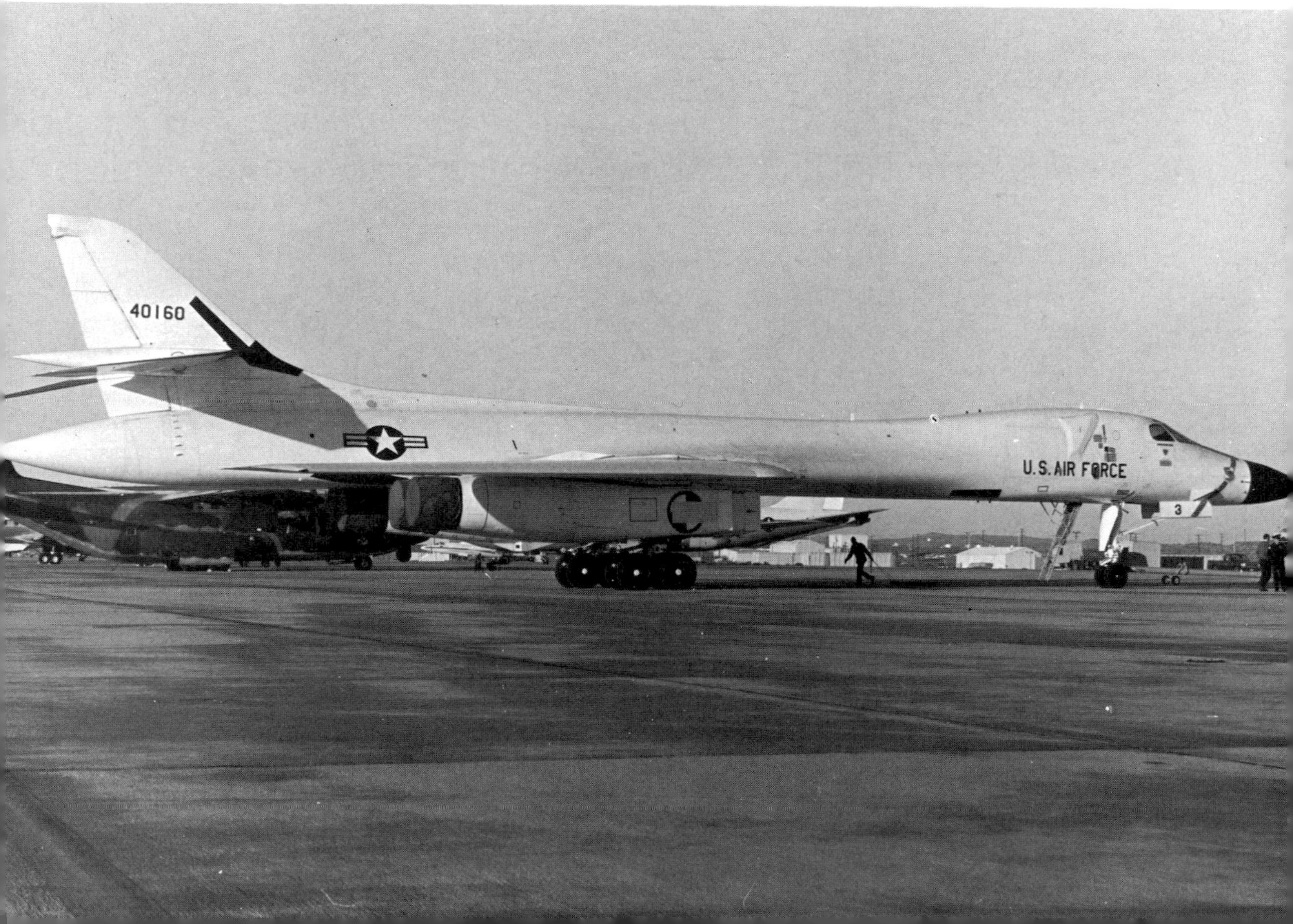

70. A number of early production F-111As are to be modified to EF-111A configuration for use in the suppression of enemy radars. These will be instantly recognizable by the prominent fin-top fairing housing antenna for the AN/ALQ-99 noise-jamming system. Two prototypes have thus far been built and it seems likely that about 40 will eventually be acquired. (Grumman Aerospace)
71. Strategic Air Command's hopes for a new bomber aircraft were dashed in the late seventies when production funding for the Rockwell B-1A was withdrawn. At least two of the four prototypes, now in a camouflage finish, are still engaged on research from Edwards AFB and a fixed-wing variant seems likely to become SAC's next manned bomber. The aircraft seen here with SAC insignia is the third prototype. However, the Reagan Administration announced in October 1981 plans for the production of 100 B1s.
72. B-52s say yes to pollution! A B-52G wends its smoky way skyward whilst a tall-tailed B-52D undergoes routine servicing at Upper Heyford during September 1976.

72▼

▲73 ▼74

75▲ 76▼

73. The open weapons bay doors are just visible in this view of B-52H 10003 of the 28th Bomb Wing at Ellsworth AFB, South Dakota. Other notable features are the open drag chute housing just behind the vertical tail surfaces, and the EVS fairings around the nose section.
74. Upper wing markings are readily apparent in this view of a 319th Bomb Wing B-52H at its home base of Grand Forks, North Dakota. The Strategic Air Command shield is just visible on the fuselage below the aft cockpit window.
75, 76. Cockpit details and upper fuselage markings can be discerned in these two views of a 319th BW B-52H Stratofortress during in-flight refuelling over North Dakota. In the lower view, both of the EVS (Electro-Optical Viewing System) sensor windows are clearly visible; this equipment comprises low-light-level television and infra-red equipment.

▲77 ▼78

77. The nose fairings for the Electro-Optical Viewing System (EVS), which was fitted to B-52Gs and B-52Hs during the seventies, are visible in this close-up view of a 28th Bomb Wing B-52H at RAF Marham. Most SAC aircraft display unit insignia to starboard, with the command badge being carried on the port side.

78. The oldest variant of the Stratofortress now active with SAC is the B-52D which, in addition to being finished in a basically black colour scheme, also differs from the G and H models in having taller vertical tail surfaces. The aircraft shown here (60683) is from the 7th Bomb Wing at Carswell AFB, Texas.

79. The spectacular Convair B-58A Hustler was in the process of being phased-out when the seventies began, having seen operational service with just two Bomb Wings since the summer of 1960. Featuring the unique dual-purpose fuel and weapons pod, B-58A 12054 carries the insignia of the 305th Bomb Wing at Bunker Hill AFB, Indiana.

80. The first seven B-58A Hustlers to be placed in storage at Davis-Monthan AFB, Arizona can be seen in this photograph, taken during November 1969. Unlike the B-52, they did not remain in store for long, almost all being scrapped during the early seventies.

79▲ 80▼

81▼ 82▶

81. SAC's principal version of the Lockheed U-2 in the seventies was the U-2R, which was considerably larger than the initial production machines, having a greater wing span and a longer fuselage. This is one of approximately seventeen aircraft of this type built in the late sixties. The slender wing and black overall finish are displayed to advantage in this in-flight study. (Lockheed)

82. The same U-2R at a later stage in its career when it had been modified to serve as a prototype for the forthcoming TR-1 tactical reconnaissance variant. The most notable external difference is the two large wing-mounted SLAR (Side-Looking Airborne Radar) pods, whilst additional aerials can be seen sprouting from various points on the fuselage. Note also that the outrigger 'pogo' wheels are still in position. (via C. Pocock)

83▲ 84▼

83. The distinctive wing planform and upper surface markings are displayed to advantage in this view of an SR-71A 'Blackbird' approaching a KC-135Q Stratotanker for in-flight refuelling. Normally based at Beale, California, SR-71As regularly operate from Kadena, Okinawa and Mildenhall, England. (USAF)

84. Lockheed's remarkable SR-71 'Blackbird' hit the headlines on several occasions in the seventies, the most notable being the record-breaking flight made between New York and London in September 1974. The aircraft seen here displays the 9th SRW badge on the fin. It was serving with Detachment One when photographed at Kadena late in 1979.

85. Used to simulate enemy aircraft and capable of jamming the defensive radar network, the EB-57B Canberra invariably wears an attractive high-visibility red and grey colour scheme. This particular example is from the Vermont ANG's 134th Defence Systems Evaluation Squadron, colloquially known as 'The Green Mountain Boys'.

86. Another old favourite which disappeared from the scene during the seventies was the Douglas B-66 Destroyer. The EB-66C, portrayed here by an aircraft from the 39th TEWS (Tactical Electronic Warfare Squadron) at Spangdahlem, West Germany, featured numerous antennae, fairings and pods for mission-related avionics.

87. The 'RC' code combination on the fin of EB-66B 30492 signifies that it served with the 41st TEWS from Takhli, as part of the 355th TFW before being retired to Davis-Monthan and scrapped.

85▲ 86▼

87▼

▲88

88. After the ceasefire in Vietnam, most surviving DHC-4A Caribou light STOL (Short Take-Off and Landing) transports passed to either the Air Force Reserve or the Air National Guard. They remained in service throughout the seventies. The aircraft depicted here was assigned to the 135th Tactical Airlift Squadron at Baltimore (Martin) Airport, Maryland, in September 1978.
89, 90. Another project which failed to reach fruition was the AMST (Advanced Medium STOL Transport), despite the fact that two prototypes of each of the two competing aircraft were flown and evaluated by the USAF. Boeing's entry (**90**), the singularly ugly YC-14, is seen here in flight in a basically natural metal finish. Its rival, the McDonnell Douglas YC-15 (**89**), wears camouflage battledress for its sole appearance at the Farnborough Air Show. (Boeing/Peacock)

89▲ 90▼

▲91 ▼92

91. The graceful contours of Boeing's Stratofreighter are clearly visible in this view of a KC-97L of the Wisconsin ANG's 126th ARS during a fly-past at Greenham Common in 1973. The auxiliary jet engine pods were a distinctive feature of this variant of the long-serving C-97.

92. One of the last Air National Guard units to operate the trusty 'Strat' was the 197th ARS at Sky Harbor Airport, Phoenix, Arizona. Like most ANG tanker squadrons, it progressed to the KC-135A Stratotanker in the latter part of the decade.

93. Having served as the backbone of the Military Air Transport Service and Military Airlift Command for many years, the C-124 Globemaster had been largely relegated to second-line units of the ANG and AFRES by the beginning of the seventies and, by 1976, had completely disappeared. The Globemaster's portly appearance is displayed to advantage in this view of a C-124C of the 436th Military Airlift Wing landing at Mildenhall in the late sixties.

94. Transport squadrons of the Air Force Reserve were almost universally equipped with the Fairchild C-119 Boxcar during the sixties, but, when the seventies opened, these were all rapidly being disposed of in favour of the Lockheed C-130 Hercules. Thereafter, only a handful of C-119Ls and AC-119s remained with the ANG and the Pacific Air Forces, and these served with a number of Special Operations Squadrons.

95. Another example of 'piston-power' which bowed-out during the decade was Lockheed's graceful Super Constellation. The last active examples were the EC-121T airborne early warning aircraft of the Air Force Reserve. The aircraft seen here is one of the rather less exotic C-121G freighters of the Pennsylvania ANG.

93▲ 94▼

95▼

▲96

96. Very few examples of the original 'Roman-nosed' C-130A Hercules now remain in regular use. This example, seen on final approach to Greenham Common for the 1979 'Hercules Meet', was from the 105th Tactical Airlift Squadron, Tennessee ANG, and carried the name 'Nashville' above the crew entry door.

97. The tactical airlift work-horse of the USAF has for long been the Lockheed Hercules and, with the abandonment of the AMST project, it looks like remaining so for some considerable time to come. This 'PR' coded machine was from the 779th TAS/464th TAW at Pope AFB. It was photographed during a routine deployment to Mildenhall prior to the December 1974 transfer of Tactical Air Command C-130 units to the Military Airlift Command, which resulted in the removal of fin code combinations.

98. One of the most interesting modifications made to the Hercules resulted in the DC-130A drone-launching version, seen here complete with a Ryan Firebee on the port inner pylon. A noteworthy feature of this aircraft is the considerably modified nose contours, which house much of the specialized drone control apparatus.

99. A predominantly grey colour scheme is worn by the WC-130 Hercules aircraft of Military Airlift Command's Air Weather Service, which are engaged on various aspects of meteorological and weather research. This machine was formerly an HC-130H and retains the unique nose contours of that variant, although the Fulton aerial snatch equipment has been removed. It is from the 53rd Weather Reconnaissance Squadron at Keesler AFB, Missouri.

▼97

98▲ 99▼

WEATHER
50985
U.S. AIR FORCE
MILITARY AIRLIFT COMMAND
53rd WRS

▲100 ▼101

100. Prior to the era of the C-5A Galaxy, MAC's heavyweight airlift aircraft was the Douglas C-133 Cargomaster, which was finally being retired in the early seventies. The aircraft seen here is a C-133B from the 60th Military Airlift Wing at Travis AFB, California, and was in fact the last of the type to be built.

101. The origins of the Lockheed C-5A Galaxy's somewhat disparaging nickname 'Fat Albert' are all too readily apparent in this fine in-flight study of the 'Marietta monster'. Military Airlift Command received a total of 81 C-5As, the survivors of which are shortly to be repainted in the so-called 'Lizard' finish first introduced on the A-10 Thunderbolt II. (Lockheed)

▲102 ▼103

▼104

102. In addition to routine in-flight refuelling, SAC also uses a number of considerably modified Stratotankers as airborne command posts and on specialized reconnaissance duties. This aircraft was one of just four RC-135D conversions, serving with the 55th Strategic Reconnaissance Wing until about 1975. Note the 'dustbin'-type nose radome and the prominent forward fuselage SLAR (Side-Looking Airborne Radar) bulges.

103. Another variant of the Stratotanker used by the 55th Strategic Reconnaissance Wing was the RC-135C, which featured turbofan engines, prominent SLAR fairings and wing-tip mounted high-frequency aerials. Ten were built, and all have been further modified to the even more bizarre RC-135U or RC-135V configuration.

104. The 55th SRW also has responsibility for SAC's 'Looking Glass' airborne command post, utilizing a number of turbofan-powered EC-135C Stratotankers in order to ensure that at least one aircraft is always airborne in the event of surprise attack.

105. The vast majority of SAC Stratotankers are standard KC-135As used for aerial refuelling of the B-52 and FB-111 manned bomber force. As single manager for the tanker fleet, SAC is also called upon to support tactical aircraft throughout the world.

106. The KC-135A depicted here, 80124, is somewhat unusual in that it is one of only a handful that possess the ability to be refuelled in-flight; this is achieved via a receptacle mounted above the cockpit. Assigned to the 55th SRW at Offutt AFB, Nebraska, it is used to train crews for the 'Looking Glass' mission.

105▲ 106▼

▲107 ▼108

109▲

107. The backbone of Military Airlift Command's long-range airlift fleet throughout the seventies was the Lockheed C-141A Starlifter, some 284 of which were originally acquired. This natural metal example carries the insignia of the 438th MAW at McGuire AFB, New Jersey.
108. By the mid-seventies the original natural metal finish of the C-141A was on the way out, with work on repainting the entire fleet in a white and grey finish having made considerable progress. An airframe stretch, adding some 23ft (7m) in length, is now underway. These modified aircraft are known as C-141Bs, and feature in-flight refuelling equipment, thus providing non-stop global capability.
109, 110. One of the cornerstones of the US military aid programme for many years has been Northrop's diminutive F-5. As part of the aid project, the Air Force provides training facilities at Williams AFB, Arizona, from where the 425th TFTS (Tactical Fighter Training Squadron) operates a mixture of F-5s, such as the F-5E (**109**) and the two-seat combat proficiency F-5B trainer variant (**110**). Both aircraft are wearing identical colour schemes; the fuselage and fin bands are painted yellow and black.

110▼

▲111 ▼112

113▲

111. In addition to the training unit, the USAF also operates a considerable number of F-5E Tiger IIs in the 'aggressor' rôle; these serve to simulate enemy aircraft in air combat manoeuvring training. A variety of different camouflage schemes are worn by such aircraft, which operate from bases in the Philippines, Britain and America. (Northrop)

112. One of the original F-5E prototypes departs from Edwards AFB during testing of the LATAR (Laser Augmented Target Acquisition and Recognition) system, which comprises a laser target designator, spot tracker and electro-optical sensor. A Maverick training missile is carried under the port wing, and AIM-9 Sidewinders are present on the wing-tip missile rails. (Northrop)

113. Advanced pilot training for the USAF has been undertaken by the Northrop T-38A Talon since the early sixties, although the seventies witnessed considerable diversification of this type's missions, when it was also used as an 'aggressor' aircraft for air combat training and as a fighter lead-in trainer. This example was attached to the ACE (Accelerated Co-Pilot Enrichment) detachment at Grand Forks in the late seventies, after temporary secondment by Air Training Command whose insignia it retains.

4
3
1
2
5
U.S. AIR FORCE
U.S. AIR FORCE
U.S. AIR FORCE
U.S. AIR FORCE
U.S. AIR FORCE
Capt Kirk Brimmer
SSgt Ray Herder

▲114 ▼115

IY
309
AFRES

116▲

114. After a number of accidents involving the F-4E Phantom, the USAF aerobatic team 'The Thunderbirds' switched to the T-38A Talon, which they still use today. Five of the team's aircraft are seen here in immaculate line-abreast formation. (Northrop)
115. Extensively used as a close air support aircraft in South-East Asia, most A-37B Dragonflies were downgraded to reserve service in 1970. This example wears the code letters and maroon fin cap of the 757th TFS/434th TFW at Youngstown Municipal Airport, Ohio. It was photographed at Willow Grove during September 1975.

116. Air Force Systems Command's Air Force Flight Test Centre (AFFTC) at Edwards AFB, California, also utilizes a number of A-37B Dragonflies for various duties associated with test and development. Most, if not all, are finished in a basically white colour scheme with day-glow red vertical tail surfaces.
117. The Dragonfly's predecessor in USAF service was the T-37, which is still in widespread use in the basic jet training rôle, although the search for a suitable replacement has begun. This natural metal T-37B was assigned to the 96th Flying Training Squadron/82nd Flying Training Wing when photographed at Williams AFB, Arizona, in 1975. Most T-37Bs are now finished in a white overall colour scheme.

117▼

118. The number of active Lockheed T-33As continued to decline throughout the seventies, and most of the surviving 100 or so aircraft are now operated by air defence dedicated squadrons of the Air National Guard and Tactical Air Command. This machine of the New York ANG's 136th FIS is seen undergoing routine maintenance at the Niagara Falls base. Its hangar-mate is one of the squadron's F-101B Voodoos.

119. Used by the Military Aircraft Storage and Disposition Centre as a hack aircraft in the late sixties and early seventies, this particular T-33A ended its days in the crash rescue compound at the Marine Corps Air Base at El Toro, California. The natural metal finish was typical of the T-33 at that time, although most were later painted light grey.

▲118 ▼119

120▲ 121▼

120. Navigation training for the USAF and the US Navy is handled by the 323rd Flying Training Wing from Mather AFB, California. The 323rd uses most of the nineteen examples of the Boeing T-43A that were acquired in the seventies. This aircraft is typical, being finished in a white top with grey undersides. ATC's badge is displayed on both sides of the vertical tail.

121. Utilized as a National Emergency Airborne Command Post (NEACP) and a SAC command post, four examples of the Boeing 747 were acquired by the USAF. Three were completed as the E-4A, while the fourth, more advanced aircraft is known as an E-4B. Additional E-4Bs are now on order, and the three E-4As are to be updated to this later standard. All are now assigned to the 55th SRW at Offutt.

▲122 ▼123

124▲

122-124. One of the newest and most sophisticated aircraft to join Tactical Air Command in recent years is the Boeing E-3A Sentry, perhaps better known as AWACS (Airborne Warning and Control System). Current USAF planning anticipates the acquisition of 34 aircraft of this type for service with the 552nd Airborne Warning and Control Wing from Tinker AFB, Oklahoma. A prominent feature of these aircraft is the huge rotodome mounted above the aft fuselage; this contains the numerous antennae for the system. Production Sentries, such as this example refuelling over West Germany, are finished in a grey overall paint scheme.

125. Employed in the dual rôle of base rescue and Minuteman or Titan missile silo support, Bell's Iroquois is mainly assigned to Military Airlift Command's Aerospace Rescue and Recovery Service (ARRS). This typical UH-1F was attached to Detachment Nine of the 37th ARRS when photographed at Grand Forks in late 1978.

125▼

▲126 ▼127

▼128

126. Kaman's distinctive Huskie was also utilized for base rescue services when the decade opened, although the surviving examples were withdrawn from use soon afterwards. Here, a natural metal HH-43F demonstrates how the downdraught from the rotor may be used to control fire during a simulated rescue at RAF Lakenheath.

127. During their final period of service, most HH-43Fs were finished in a grey overall colour scheme. This example features standard Military Airlift Command insignia. Other noteworthy aspects are the loudspeakers on the extreme nose section, and the unusual undercarriage.

128. Extensively used in South-East Asia, the Sikorsky HH-53C still serves as the principal long-range rescue helicopter around the world. This aircraft, seen here in low-visibility markings, is from the Eglin-based 55th Aerospace Rescue and Recovery Service, and is making its final approach to Hurlburt Field, part of the massive Eglin complex.